AIDS:
Answers to Questions Kids Ask

Written by Barbara Christie-Dever
Illustrated by Marcy Ramsey

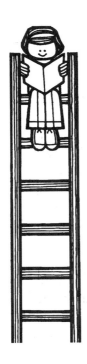

Cover design by Andy Blinn

Illustrations by Marcy Ramsey

Typesetting and editorial production by Clark Editorial & Design

Dedication

To my sons Greg, Jeff, Marc, and Mike,
who are among my best teachers.

Acknowledgments

I would like to express my appreciation to the many courteous and caring people who staff the HIV/AIDS hotlines and information services administered by federal, state, and local agencies. Special thanks to the Centers for Disease Control and Prevention (CDC) National HIV/AIDS Clearinghouse for providing many informative documents and to CDC information specialist, Michael La Flamm.

Much gratitude goes to the following health care professionals and HIV-prevention educators who thoroughly and candidly reviewed the manuscript and provided valuable insights from their professional perspectives: Lisa DiRicco, a middle school health teacher; Gloria Johnson, a community HIV-prevention educator specializing in high-risk youth; Susan King, a licensed MFCC specializing in school programs for children and teens; and Gregory Thomas, M.D., M.P.H., Health Officer for San Luis Obispo County, California, and Director of the Family Care Center for San Luis Obispo General Hospital.

Many thanks also to my wonderful family for their continued patience and support of my writing.

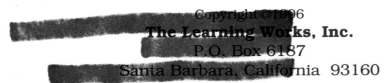

Copyright © 1996
The Learning Works, Inc.
P.O. Box 6187
Santa Barbara, California 93160
ISBN: 0-88160-286-8

A Note to Teachers and Parents

AIDS: Answers to Questions Kids Ask was written specifically for middle school students. The book begins with basic facts about HIV—the virus that destroys the human immune system and thereby brings about the condition we call AIDS. It explains how the virus is transmitted from one person to another and provides information about HIV testing and treatment. The reader is reminded that there is no cure for AIDS; there is no vaccine against HIV. The only hope that this epidemic can be stopped lies in prevention—and the greatest challenge of prevention relies on the involvement of kids about to become teens.

This book explains that HIV/AIDS is a preventable disease. It encourages sexual abstinence and staying off drugs. It stresses learning effective communication, decision-making, and assertiveness skills and advises kids on how to talk about sexual abstinence. It does not suggest condom use for this age group, but describes condoms as the best protection against HIV for older, sexually-active people.

Extended activities and lists of additional resources for more information are provided to enhance the learning experience and to help kids make healthy choices through their teen and young adult years.

Since this book is addressed to kids who are at different levels of development, some readers may need assistance with the more advanced material. All kids, however, are encouraged to read this book and to use it as a stimulus for peer discussion and interaction.

A Note to Kids

AIDS is a serious disease. There is no cure for it and there is no vaccine against HIV, the virus that causes AIDS. But many people still do the two primary things that transmit HIV to others. People still have unprotected sex and share needles to inject drugs. It is estimated that 1 in every 250 Americans has already been infected with HIV and more people are being infected every day.

As a young person about to become a teenager, you need to be concerned because teens are now getting infected with HIV at a faster rate than any other age group. You will need to be careful because you won't be able to tell who is infected and who isn't. In most cases, HIV doesn't cause a person to feel sick for a long time—sometimes years. A person infected with HIV can look and act just as healthy as someone who is not infected.

To protect yourself against HIV/AIDS, you need to be informed. You may already know some things about HIV and AIDS, but you need to learn more. You also need to explore some of the issues related to HIV, such as sex, relationships, drugs, and discrimination. Most importantly, you need to start now to make sure that you will have a strong foundation of facts and values, as well as decision-making and communication skills, to make the best possible choices for yourself.

This book covers some advanced topics and discusses some experiences that you may have not yet encountered. It also contains some terminology that you might not be familiar with. Words that appear in boldface type within the text are defined in a glossary at the end of the book. Ask for help when you need it. Think about how what you learn could affect your life. The activities in the "On Your Own" and "Extended Activities" sections have been included to help you prepare for real-life situations more effectively. This book also contains profiles of well-known people who have been diagnosed with HIV/AIDS.

Contents

Contents

(continued)

What is AIDS? What causes AIDS?

AIDS stands for **a**cquired **i**mmune **d**eficiency **s**yndrome. Acquired immune deficiency syndrome is a condition in which the body's **immune system** becomes so deficient, or damaged, that it can no longer defend the body against microorganisms that can cause disease. People with AIDS die of illnesses that normally do not threaten people whose immune systems are complete and strong.

Scientists have learned that the weakened immune system that leads to AIDS is caused by a **virus**. This virus is called **HIV**, an acronym that stands for **h**uman **i**mmunodeficiency **v**irus. This virus has the ability to enter certain cells of the immune system, disable them, and use them to make more viruses. These cells are called **CD4 cells**, T4 cells, or T-helper cells.

People who are infected with HIV usually do not have recognizable **symptoms** for several years—even as many as ten or more years. Nevertheless, the virus is at work destroying CD4 cells and making more deadly viruses. When large numbers of CD4 cells have been destroyed, people with HIV are said to have developed AIDS. People with AIDS develop many health problems. These can include extreme weight loss, severe pneumonia and other infections, certain forms of cancer, and damage to the nervous system, which can cause mental and emotional problems.

Many people have been infected with HIV and don't know it, and they can infect others without knowing it. HIV is almost always spread by sexual contact or by sharing needles used to inject drugs. It cannot be spread by everyday, casual contact because HIV cannot live outside certain human body fluids.

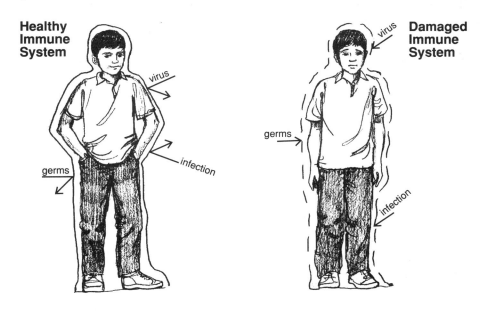

When and where did AIDS start?

AIDS was first observed in the United States in 1981. At that time, no one knew what was causing it. Early that year, doctors at a large hospital in Los Angeles had begun to notice similarities among the conditions of three young men who had been admitted to the hospital within days of each other.

They all were severely ill with infections that seldom occurred in healthy people. Later that year, more young men in Los Angeles, as well as in other major cities such as San Francisco, New York, and Miami, came down with similar illnesses. Some of them also had a rare cancer that had previously affected only a few elderly men.

Doctors who were treating these patients noticed that they all were suffering from a severe **immune system deficiency** that appeared to be causing a common **syndrome**, or group of symptoms. They suspected that a previously unknown virus might be responsible for damaging the immune systems of these patients.

In 1983, two research doctors, one in the United States and one in France, discovered the virus that doctors had been searching for. Dr. Luc Montagnier at the Pasteur Institute in Paris announced his discovery first, and Dr. Robert Gallo of the National Cancer Institute in the United States showed that the newly-isolated virus was the one causing AIDS.

Scientists now believe that HIV was first introduced to North America in the mid- to late-1970s. At first, it was thought that AIDS was confined to homosexual males, but soon it was learned that recipients of blood and blood products and people who had used needles to inject drugs were also getting AIDS. Later, AIDS began to appear in people who had sexual contact with these first three groups and in babies born to infected mothers.

It is not known for certain where HIV originated, but blood samples taken in Africa as early as 1959 have been found to contain evidence of the virus. HIV has now spread to virtually every country on earth. In the United States, AIDS is considered an *epidemic,* a disease that has spread to a large portion of the country's population. Worldwide, AIDS is a *pandemic* disease, having reached people in nearly every country on the earth.

On Your Own

Do research to learn more about the history of HIV.

How many people have AIDS? HIV?

Since 1981, the Centers for Disease Control and Prevention (CDC) in Atlanta, Georgia, has been keeping track of the numbers of AIDS and HIV cases in the United States. All of the states are required to report AIDS cases, but not all are required to report HIV cases (people who have been infected with HIV, but who have not yet developed AIDS). Some states do, however, report the number of HIV cases, but generally these are the states with the fewest cases. This leaves a large number of HIV cases out of the statistics. HIV statistics reflect only the "tip of the iceberg."

Every June and December, the CDC compiles *reported* AIDS and HIV cases in a detailed statistical report. On November 24, 1995, however, the CDC issued a special report because the number of reported AIDS cases in this country had exceeded 500,000. As of October 31, 1995, a total of 501,310 AIDS cases had been reported since 1981. According to CDC figures, more than 62 percent of these people (311,381) have died, and 189,929 people are currently living with AIDS in this country. Because new statistics tend to be incomplete, we can assume that there are considerably more actual cases.

CDC statistics show that about 20 percent of all AIDS cases are diagnosed in people ages 20 to 29. Because experts know that it takes an average of seven to ten years for an HIV-infected person to develop AIDS, they also know that most of the people diagnosed with AIDS at ages 20 to 29 were infected with HIV when they were teens.

CDC statistics also show that HIV infection has been increasing and continues to increase in teens faster than in any other group. Again, no one knows how many people are actually infected with HIV. The CDC has estimated, however, that 1 in 250 (about one million) Americans is infected with HIV. The World Health Organization estimates that 20 million people worldwide have been infected with HIV.

How is HIV spread from one person to another?

HIV gets into the body by means of an infected person's body fluids—mainly blood, **semen**, **preseminal fluid**, and **vaginal secretions**. It can also be transmitted from an infected mother to her infant through breast milk, as well as by blood before and during childbirth when the baby's blood and the mother's blood are in direct contact. HIV is almost always passed from one person to another through sexual contact and sharing IV drug needles.

- **Sexual contact**

  HIV infection is a **sexually transmitted disease (STD)**. HIV can be **transmitted** (passed from one person to another) during any kind of sexual contact that involves blood, semen, preseminal fluid, or vaginal secretions. This includes **sexual intercourse** (vaginal and **anal**) as well as **oral sex**. Although a cut, tear, or sore on the penis, vagina, rectum, or mouth can increase the risk of infection, HIV can also penetrate healthy **mucous membranes**, especially in the vagina and rectum. (Transmission of HIV through sexual contact is further described on page 22.)

- **Sharing IV drug needles**

  IV stands for **intravenous**, which means entering by way of a vein. HIV can live in the small amount of blood that always remains in an IV drug needle and syringe after use. It is a known fact that most IV drug users share needles. Blood also remains in needles and syringes used to inject vitamins or steroids (muscle-building drugs). Having sex with someone who injects drugs is extremely risky. (Transmission of HIV through sharing IV drug needles is further described on page 23.)

There are other ways that HIV can enter the body, but these ways rarely occur. HIV infection from blood transfusions, organ or bone marrow transplants, and artificial insemination is extremely rare today because all donors are pretested for HIV. Health care workers have been accidentally stuck with infected needles, but revised procedures generally prevent such accidents. Dentists also follow strict safety and sterilization procedures. HIV can possibly enter the body from traces of blood on unsterilized instruments used for ear piercing, tattooing, and acupuncture, but, as of this writing, no cases have been documented.

Can anyone get HIV, the virus that causes AIDS?

Yes. Anyone can become infected with HIV: infants, children, teens, parents, grandparents; the rich and the poor; people of any race, religion, or country; people of any **sexual orientation**; and people in any job.

In recent years, new cases of AIDS have been leveling off and possibly decreasing among **homosexual** and **bisexual** males and increasing among **heterosexual** people. This change is showing up statistically as an increase in the number of new cases of HIV and AIDS in women and teens and also, until recently, as an increase in the number of new cases in infants and children. New cases in children have stopped increasing because scientists have discovered that the drug AZT can prevent pregnant women infected with HIV from transmitting the virus to their unborn babies.

When you hear or read about what "groups" are getting HIV, it is important to remember that it is not what group you are in, but what you *do* that will determine whether or not you will get HIV. Although it is true that anyone can get the virus, it is not easy to get (like a cold, flu, or even measles or chicken pox). In fact, you cannot become infected with HIV unless you do certain high-risk things.

People who have unprotected sex and people who share IV drug needles are at highest risk of **contracting** HIV. These two activities are so risky that having sex just one time with an HIV-infected person or using an unsterile IV needle only once can result in infection.

PROFILE: Ryan White

Until Ryan White discovered he had been infected by HIV, he was a typical kid growing up in a small Indiana town called Kokomo. He did, however, have a disease called hemophilia, which prevented his blood from clotting. Since his birth on December 6, 1971, Ryan had received regular injections of a blood product called Factor VIII to help his blood clot normally. Without it, he would have bled to death from a minor cut or bruise.

Although Ryan's parents divorced when he was six, he had a very close, happy home life with his younger sister, Andrea, and their mom, Jeanne. Ryan regularly read *Time* magazine with his grandpa. It was there that he first learned about AIDS in 1982.

One day in August of 1984, Ryan's grandpa expressed his concern that maybe Ryan could get HIV from the Factor VIII. Ryan had told him not to worry, but later that year, after having bouts of diarrhea and stomach cramps, nights sweats, and finally a case of pneumocystis pneumonia just before Christmas, Ryan was diagnosed with AIDS.

After spending two months in the hospital, Ryan was allowed to go home. By the spring, he was feeling better. When he was ready to go back to school, however, school personnel informed Ryan and his family that he would not be allowed to return. The teachers and parents were afraid that they or their kids would get HIV. Ryan begged his mother to do something—to fight back. While she was trying to figure out what to do, a local TV station showed up at their house with cameras and reporters. Ryan got his first chance to protest being banned from school on live TV!

Finally, the school offered Ryan a two-way speaker phone hookup between his house and the school. Ryan's mom said they'd try it, but it didn't work very well. Ryan wanted to be in the classroom. Back in August, Ryan's mom had gone to court to get an order from the judge saying that Ryan had a right to be in school. The judge had said they needed to come back in November with proof that he had been banned from school. In November, the judge ruled that the school had no legal grounds to keep Ryan from attending, but the school board planned to appeal the ruling.

After two more trips to the hospital and several appearances on national television news and talk shows, Ryan's first day back at school arrived. He was met by news reporters and students with picket signs reading, "Students Against AIDS." Before the day was over, Ryan was pulled out of class and told by the principal that he had to go back to court because a concerned parents group was threatening to sue Ryan's parents, his doctor, and the school for taking him back. This time, the judge ordered that Ryan temporarily be kept from attending school.

In the months that followed, Ryan and his family were taunted by nasty editorials, annoying and threatening phone calls, and even a bullet hole through their front window. In April of 1985, a state court overturned the lower court's temporary order barring Ryan from school. Within an hour, Ryan was back in school, but he was shunned by nearly everyone. That summer, he was banned from the public swimming pools. Ryan had had enough; he wanted to move.

The family was broke from all the medical bills, but a company in Los Angeles that had wanted to make a TV movie about Ryan offered enough money up front to pay for a new house in a small town called Cicero, about an hour's drive south of Kokomo. The family moved in May of 1985. From that point on, Ryan was happier. He had new friends and a school that welcomed him. He met lots of celebrities on trips to California and became a loved and respected AIDS educator in demand all over the country. For the next four years, in between bouts of illness and trips around the country for public appearances, Ryan was able to enjoy just being a teenager. Ryan White died on April 8, 1990, at the age of 18.

Follow-up Activities

The following questions are based on the book, *Ryan White: My Own Story*. (See page 59 for information on this book.)

1. What do you think was the most important point that Ryan White made in his March 1988 presentation to the President's Commission on AIDS? (See pages 257–260.)

2. What important piece of legislation is dedicated to the memory of Ryan White? (See pages 252–253.)

3. What part did Ryan White play in the movie, *The Ryan White Story*? How did Ryan feel about playing the part? (See pages 121, 171, and 185.)

What happens when HIV gets into a person's body?

The body's first lines of defense against any type of disease-causing **microorganism** are the skin and mucous membranes. Certain mucous membranes are more susceptible to penetration by HIV than others, and even slightly irritated skin can allow HIV to enter. The facts that (1) HIV is carried in semen, preseminal fluid, and vaginal secretions, and (2) that the mucous membranes of the vagina and rectum are particularly susceptible to HIV help to explain why HIV is transmitted sexually.

Once past the skin or mucous membrane, HIV, like most viruses, enters and remains in the bloodstream until it recognizes the certain kinds of cells it can enter. Normally, your body is ready with an army of specialized **white blood cells** that are part of its complex immune system to protect the body's cells from being invaded by disease-causing microorganisms. The primary types of white blood cells are (1) **lymphocytes** (also called T cells and B cells), which identify substances as foreign and build defenses called **antibodies** against them, and (2) large **phagocytes**, which surround and destroy the invading microorganisms.

HIV enters a special lymphocyte called a **CD4 cell**, which normally directs other cells to find and destroy foreign substances like viruses. When HIV recognizes a CD4 cell, HIV enters the cell and uses it to **replicate** (make exact copies of) HIV. When the cell is full of new viruses, it bursts, releasing the new viruses into the bloodstream to find new CD4 cells to invade. The original cell usually dies.

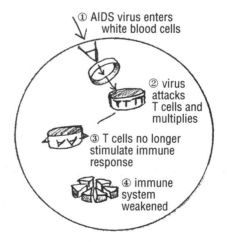

① AIDS virus enters white blood cells
② virus attacks T cells and multiplies
③ T cells no longer stimulate immune response
④ immune system weakened

As CD4 cells are killed, the immune system grows weaker and eventually breaks down completely. When the immune system is seriously damaged, other microorganisms that don't normally hurt healthy people can cause serious, life-threatening diseases in people with HIV.

Can people tell
if they are infected with HIV?

No, not at first. People don't realize that they have been infected with HIV because they may not notice any initial symptoms, or they may simply think that they have the flu. Approximately 14 days following infection with HIV, many people experience flu-like symptoms that last about two weeks. These initial symptoms may include chills, fever, fatigue, headache, swollen glands, rash, and diarrhea. There is nothing peculiar about these symptoms to distinguish them from those caused by many cold and flu viruses.

Following these initial symptoms, a person infected with HIV generally will have no further symptoms for months or years. He or she is said to be **asymptomatic**. The only way doctors can tell if a person is infected is by testing his or her blood for the presence of HIV antibodies.

In most cases, people who are infected have no idea that anything is wrong until the disease has progressed to a point at which a wide range of recurrent symptoms begin to appear. As HIV inflicts more and more damage upon the immune system, infected people experience increased symptoms because they are becoming more susceptible to certain **opportunistic infections (OIs)** and rare **AIDS-related cancers** that healthy people are able to resist.

During this pre-AIDS stage of HIV infection (called **HIV illness**), people may have recurrent or prolonged intestinal, lung, and skin infections caused by common bacteria, viruses, fungi, or **parasites**. **Thrush** is a common **yeast**, or fungal, infection that affects the mouth. **Tuberculosis (TB)** is a bacterial lung infection that can reactivate during HIV illness in people who have previously had it. Often, people do not learn that they have been infected with HIV until opportunistic illnesses begin to appear.

What are some of the early symptoms of HIV infection?

The symptoms of early HIV infection are not usually recognized as such because many of them are similar to symptoms of common illnesses. The main differences between the symptoms of HIV infection and the symptoms of common illnesses are that the symptoms of HIV infection last much longer, recur often, and are more severe than those of common illnesses.

Some of the symptoms that can indicate *possible* HIV infection are

- frequent or long-term diarrhea with no apparent cause

- swollen glands in several parts of the body for no known reason

- rapid weight loss of ten or more pounds that is not the result of dieting

- high fevers (103 degrees or more) that last more than five days

- sores or infections that do not go away after medical treatment

- unexplained fatigue or weakness that lasts for weeks or months

- repeated and frequent cold or flu-like symptoms that last for days

- a cough that brings up fluid from the lungs and lasts for several weeks

- a recurrent or long-lasting white coating in the mouth

- prolonged night sweats with no apparent cause

These are only some of the symptoms that can indicate HIV infection. If a person has one or more of these symptoms, it does not necessarily mean that he or she has HIV. By the same token, if a person does not have any of these symptoms, it does not necessarily mean that he or she does not have HIV. The only way for people who have had unprotected sex or used IV drugs to know whether they have HIV is to be tested.

What are the symptoms of AIDS?

According to the CDC, everyone who has HIV will probably develop AIDS at some point. On the average, it takes from seven to ten years from the time of infection with HIV for AIDS to develop. At this point, the immune system is unable to prevent common microorganisms from infecting the body. The symptoms of AIDS depend on which micro-organisms are gaining the upper hand.

In a person with AIDS, diarrhea frequently becomes intolerable; weight loss often becomes extreme; a rare and severe form of pneumonia (*Pneumocystis carinii* **pneumonia**, or **PCP**) might cause severe fatigue and coughing; the skin and mucous membranes of the mouth and throat may become severely infected with a normally harmless, white fungus called *Candida albicans*; and unusual brown or red spots may appear on the skin, caused by cancers such as **Kaposi's sarcoma**.

People with opportunistic infections that affect the brain may lose their ability to speak or walk, or may become confused or experience memory loss. People with opportunistic infections that affect the eyes may lose their sight.

On Your Own

Do research to learn more about AIDS symptoms and some of the AIDS-related cancers and opportunistic infections that cause them. In addition to the resources available at your local library, you can check for articles on the Internet or get information from a local AIDS service organization (look under "AIDS" in the "Community Services" section in the front of your telephone directory). Information can also be obtained from the CDC National AIDS Clearinghouse (see page 56).

Is there a cure for AIDS?

No, there is no cure for AIDS. Most people with AIDS will die from AIDS-related cancers and OIs. There are, however, drugs that do three basic things: (1) slow down the replication of HIV, (2) help to rebuild the damaged immune system, and (3) treat or prevent opportunistic infections and AIDS-related cancers.

- **Antiretroviral drugs**
  Eight antiretroviral drugs have been approved by the Federal Drug Administration (FDA): AZT, ddI, ddC, d4T, 3TC, saquinavir, ritonavir, and indinavir. 3TC has been shown to strengthen and lengthen the effectiveness of AZT and to elevate the T cell counts of some patients. Saquinavir, ritonavir, and indinavir interrupt the replication of HIV at a later stage than the other five. Thus, administering saquinavir, ritonavir, and indinavir with one of the other five can deal the virus a "one-two punch."

- **Immunomodulator drugs**
  Immunomodulators—drugs that help the immune system work better—have been approved by the FDA and are prescribed by doctors. Interferon, for example, is a drug that helps fight the AIDS-related cancer, Kaposi's sarcoma. Another immunomodulator, immune globulin intravenous, often called IGIV, helps children with AIDS resist serious bacterial infections.

- **OI drugs**
  A large number of drugs are available to treat opportunistic infections associated with AIDS. OI drugs help patients by treating severe infections; keeping chronic, or long-term, infections in check; and preventing new infections. Many of the newer OI drugs are the preventive kind. One OI drug, for example, can prevent the AIDS-related pneumonia, PCP. Another can prevent reactivation of tuberculosis.

On Your Own

Dial up the electronic bulletin board system (BBS) of the Food and Drug Administration (FDA) on a computer (see page 56) to learn about recently-approved AIDS drugs.

Is there a vaccine to prevent HIV?

No. As of this writing, there is no **vaccine** for preventing HIV infection. Will there ever be a vaccine that can boost a person's immunity to HIV before the person comes in contact with the virus? Theoretically yes, but many experts think that scientists are years away from developing a successful vaccine because of HIV's ability to **mutate**, or change itself, so rapidly.

A vaccine that works against one strain, or type, of HIV may not work against another. Also, the HIV antibodies made by the human immune system are not able to kill the virus. Therefore, unless a vaccine can stimulate the immune system to make more effective antibodies, an HIV vaccine may not work.

Because of the many problems involved in finding a cure or vaccine, preventing people from becoming infected in the first place is the best hope for stopping the spread of HIV infection.

There is, however, still hope that one day scientists will be able to **genetically** engineer a vaccine or genetically manipulate the immune system so that it can eradicate this deadly virus.

On Your Own

Do research to learn how vaccines were developed to eliminate smallpox and polio.

PROFILE: Arthur Ashe

Arthur Ashe was the first African-American athlete to break into the world of professional tennis. As a young boy in Richmond, Virginia, Arthur had learned to live with segregation. He attended an all-black school and played in an all-black park. In 1947, when Arthur was four years old, his father was hired as a special police officer in Richmond's largest park. Along with the job came the family's new home, located on the park grounds. Nearby were baseball fields, a swimming pool, and tennis courts. Arthur was small, but he loved sports.

Arthur learned the importance of hard work and self-discipline from his father and the love of books and reading from his mother. At age seven, Arthur became interested in tennis. He had fast reflexes and learned the game quickly. At age ten, Arthur had won a park tournament.

Arthur kept improving his game and entering tournaments. Even though the Supreme Court had ruled against segregation in 1954, there was still a good deal of resistance to integration. Arthur was prevented from entering many tournaments and was shunned at others. Despite the racial barriers, Arthur began moving up in the ranks of young tennis players. At age 12, he was ranked the best player in the country for his age group. At 14, he entered the National Junior Championships; at 16, he made his debut at the 1959 United States National Championships; and at 17, he became the youngest winner of the American Tennis Association (ATA) junior and men's titles.

In order to keep training during the winter, Arthur moved to St. Louis, Missouri, for his senior year of high school. In 1960, Arthur won the U.S. Lawn Tennis Association national title. Arthur Ashe graduated from high school with the highest grade point average in his class and was awarded a scholarship to the University of California at Los Angeles. At UCLA, Arthur studied business administration and worked with one of the country's best tennis coaches, J. D. Morgan.

By 1965, Arthur had become the best college tennis player in the United States. After graduating from college at age 23, Arthur spent two years in the army, emerging as a first lieutenant. He later became the number-two amateur tennis player in the country. In 1968, Arthur won both the United States National and United States Open singles titles—something no one else had ever done. Winning these two titles placed him in

PROFILE: Arthur Ashe

the number one position. By 1974, however, Arthur had slipped to number five. He was determined to regain the number one position. He succeeded by winning the World Tennis Championships that year and Wimbledon the following year.

In 1977, at age 34, Arthur married Jeanne Marie Moutoussamy. In the summer of 1979, Arthur suffered a heart attack. In December of that year, he underwent successful heart surgery. Although his tennis playing days were over, Arthur continued as captain of the U.S. Davis Cup team from 1981 to 1984. He also took on new challenges. He served as campaign chairperson for the American Heart Association and helped to educate people about heart disease. In 1981, he wrote his third autobiography, *Off the Court*, and his own tennis instruction book. Following another heart surgery in 1983, Ashe continued work on his greatest book, *A Hard Road to Glory*, a three-volume history of black American athletes, which was published in 1988.

In 1987, Arthur and Jeanne were blessed with a daughter, Camera. In 1988, Arthur discovered that he had been infected with HIV during his 1983 heart surgery. He publicly announced that he had AIDS in 1992, the year he founded the Arthur Ashe Foundation for the Defeat of AIDS. Arthur Ashe died on February 7, 1993, of pneumonia, a complication of AIDS. He is remembered as an athlete who made history on the tennis courts, and as a man who worked hard to help others.

Follow-up Activities

Do research to answer the following questions about the many contributions Arthur Ashe made to society. (Complete information on the source books referred to below can be found on page 59.)

1. What was Arthur Ashe's real challenge as the first black man to be invited to compete in the South African Open? (Source: *Arthur Ashe and His Match with History*, page 27.)

2. What fundraising event is held annually by the Arthur Ashe Foundation? Who participates? (Source: *Jet* magazine, September 19, 1994, page 48.)

3. List some of the awards and invitations that Arthur Ashe received in 1992 for his humanitarian efforts. (Source: *Days of Grace: A Memoir*, pages 268–269.)

4. Why did Arthur Ashe have a brain operation on September 8, 1988? What did the doctors find? What did it mean? (Source: *Days of Grace: A Memoir*, pages 196–204.)

How do most people become infected with HIV?

Most people become infected with HIV through unprotected sexual intercourse with an infected person. HIV can be spread by any kind of sexual intercourse—vaginal, anal, and oral; homosexual and hetero-sexual. All that is required is intimate sexual contact with an HIV-infected person. In most cases, people are infected with HIV through contact with people who look perfectly healthy and who are unaware that they have HIV in their bodies.

You may have heard that HIV can only be spread by certain kinds of sexual intercourse, or that females cannot pass HIV to males, or that a person cannot get HIV unless he or she has an open sore or irritation on the sex organs. None of the preceding statements is true.

It is true that some kinds of sexual intercourse can spread HIV more easily than others. Anal intercourse is more risky than vaginal intercourse because the mucous membranes of the rectum are drier and more likely to tear than those of the vagina. Vaginal intercourse is more risky than oral sex, but vaginal or oral bleeding increases the risk of HIV transmission during oral sex.

On Your Own

Test your knowledge of how HIV is spread through sexual intercourse. On a separate piece of paper, answer the following questions. Check your own answers by rereading this page.

1. How do most people contract HIV?
2. Can you usually tell if someone is infected with HIV?
3. Can HIV be contracted only through certain kinds of sexual intercourse?
4. Is there any risk of contracting HIV through oral sex?
5. Is there more risk of contracting HIV through vaginal or anal sex?

How Most People Contract HIV
(continued)

The second most common way that HIV is spread is by sharing needles to inject IV drugs. Most IV drug users share needles and are at high risk of becoming infected with HIV. Intravenous drug users transmit HIV in two ways.

The first way is by using a needle and syringe after another person has used it. An IV drug user finds a vein by drawing a little blood into the needle before injecting the drug. This always leaves blood in the needle and syringe. If the person is HIV infected, the next person to use the needle will inject some of the infected blood directly into his or her bloodstream. It is not the drug that contains HIV; it is the previous user's blood.

The second way IV drug users spread HIV is by passing the virus to their partner during sexual intercourse. Many times neither partner knows they are infected until their baby is born infected with HIV.

If a pregnant woman who has HIV is given AZT during her pregnancy, there is a good chance that her baby will not contract the virus. Some states now require pregnant women to have their blood tested for signs of HIV infection. If HIV antibodies are detected, treatment with AZT is started immediately.

On Your Own

Test your knowledge of how IV drug users transmit HIV. Answer the following questions on a separate piece of paper. Check your answers by rereading this page and page 10.

1. Do certain drugs contain HIV?
2. What does IV stand for?
3. What is always left behind in an IV drug user's needle and syringe?
4. Can IV drug users transmit HIV sexually?
5. How does an IV drug user's baby become infected with HIV?

What are some misconceptions about how HIV is spread?

Through fear and lack of accurate information, some people believe that HIV is transmitted by everyday contact with other people or their environment. To help dispel some of these misconceptions and resulting myths, study the following list.

Ways That HIV Is <u>Not</u> Transmitted:

- holding hands, hugging, touching, talking, playing
- kissing someone on the cheek or lips
- being exposed to coughs or sneezes
- sharing food or drinking out of the same glass or soda can
- eating in a restaurant, being in a crowd, attending school
- sharing towels, washcloths, or napkins
- using public telephones, toilets, swimming pools, hot tubs, or showers
- being stung by an insect or bitten by an animal
- touching someone's tears, sweat, or saliva

No scientific evidence has ever been found to support HIV infection by any of the above means. HIV simply cannot survive outside of certain human body fluids. Any case of HIV infection that suggests the possibility of a previously unknown route of HIV transmission is promptly and thoroughly investigated by state and local health departments with assistance from the CDC.

On Your Own

Write down some of your honest feelings about being around people with HIV or AIDS. Consider, for example, how you would feel about playing a board game with an AIDS patient, sharing a soda with an HIV-positive friend, or baby-sitting for an infant with AIDS.

Can French kissing spread HIV?

There is a theoretical possibility that HIV could be transmitted during French kissing, that is, putting one's tongue in another person's mouth while kissing. The CDC considers this possible but extremely unlikely and, as of this writing, there have been no confirmed instances in which HIV was transmitted solely by kissing of any kind.

Although minute quantities of HIV have been detected in some AIDS patients' saliva and tears, research scientists and physicians concur that transmission of HIV by these fluids is highly unlikely, if not impossible. There have been no reported cases of HIV transmission by saliva or tears.

Remember that HIV is transmitted by blood. Any blood present during kissing, such as from bleeding gums or a cut or sore on the mouth, lips, or other part of the body, will increase the risk of HIV transmission.

On Your Own

For more information on how HIV is and is not transmitted, request the CDC bulletin, "Facts About the Human Immunodeficiency Virus and its Transmission." (See page 56 for the address of the CDC National AIDS Clearinghouse.)

Has an athlete ever contracted HIV from a sports injury?

No. As of this writing, no incidence of HIV transmission has ever been traced to a sports injury. There is, however, a *theoretical* risk of HIV transmission from an HIV-infected player to a noninfected player if there is bloody contact during athletic practice or competition. But studies released by the CDC in February of 1995 indicate that the risk is "extremely low."

In spite of the extremely low risk, several publications outline universal precautions for handling blood from a sports-related injury. These include Occupational Safety and Health Administration (OSHA) regulations, CDC guidelines, and the NCAA Sports Medicine Handbook. Coaches, trainers, sports doctors, and athletes should be familiar with and follow these precautions.

There is, however, a high risk of HIV infection for any athlete who shares needles or syringes to inject steroids, hormones, or vitamins. Sharing needles or syringes even once presents a significant risk of becoming infected with HIV because the virus can remain in the needle or syringe and then be injected into the next person who uses it.

An area of concern for older kids may be the dilemma of whether to administer first aid or CPR to an injured person, especially if he or she is the only person present at the scene. The American Red Cross has prepared instructions and classes to teach people how to handle such situations without putting themselves at risk of HIV infection.

On Your Own

Ask your coach or physical education teacher to explain to you and your class or team the universal precautions that should be taken when dealing with a sports injury involving blood.

Has anyone become infected by donating blood?

Donating blood has always been safe because only new, sterilized, and packaged needles and syringes are used. After they are used, the needles and syringes are promptly discarded and destroyed. There is no possible way to come in contact with the AIDS virus by donating blood at a blood bank. (The same procedures apply to any type of injection (shot) a patient might receive in a health care setting.)

Receiving blood, however, has not always been safe. Before March of 1985, blood and blood products could not be tested for signs of HIV infection and, as a result, a considerable number of adults, children, and babies became infected through receiving blood transfusions.

In March of 1985, the **HIV antibody test** was developed. This test can detect HIV antibodies, the immune system's defense against HIV, in the blood of HIV-infected people. If HIV antibodies are found in any donated blood, the blood is discarded so that it can never be used.

Contracting HIV through receiving a blood transfusion is nearly impossible today because all blood donors are tested. A slight risk is due to a very small number of donors who haven't had HIV long enough for their bodies to produce antibodies found by testing. The "window period" for the body to produce HIV antibodies ranges from about two weeks to six months.

For this reason, people who are at highest risk of HIV infection—IV drug users, their sexual partners, and people who have multiple sexual partners—are advised not to give blood. Blood banks use screening procedures that usually involve asking potential donors a series of questions designed to screen out high-risk individuals.

On Your Own

The blood product used to treat hemophilia, a disease in which the blood does not clot, is made from the blood of hundreds of different donors. This is why many hemophiliacs became infected with HIV before 1985. Do research at the library or on the Internet to learn more about hemophilia.

PROFILE: Magic Johnson

Earvin "Magic" Johnson was born in Lansing, Michigan, on August 14, 1959. He was the middle child of seven children born to Earvin and Christine Johnson. Earvin Sr. worked in an automobile plant and also operated his own cleaning-and-hauling business. Christine worked as a school custo-dian in addition to being a full-time mother and homemaker.

Young Earvin loved to play basketball more than anything else. Earvin Sr. had been a good basketball player in high school. Earvin Jr. and his father would watch NBA games on television and then go outside to practice what they had seen. Earvin's father called him Junior. Junior learned many important lessons about the game of basketball and the value of hard work from his father. During their practice games, Earvin's father taught him that a good basketball player had to know how to play all the positions equally well.

Earvin took his basketball everywhere and practiced every chance he got. He would even go to school two hours early to play before the bell rang. He started playing in organized leagues in the fourth grade. He was so much better than his peers that he would often watch older kids play. Soon he was playing in their games. By seventh grade, city newspaper reporters were writing about Earvin regularly. After one high school game in which Earvin had outplayed even himself, a reporter asked him if he could give Earvin the nickname "Magic."

Magic went on to lead his teammates to many championships in high school, college, the NBA, and finally the Olympic Games. With the Los Angeles Lakers, Magic won five NBA titles and three Most Valuable Player awards. His teammates loved and respected him for his winning smile, positive attitude, and his unselfish love of the game. To Magic, passing the ball for an assist was just as good as making the basket himself.

When Magic Johnson learned in October of 1991 that he had been infected with the AIDS virus, he first made sure that his new wife, Earleatha ("Cookie"), and their unborn baby were not infected. Cookie's test came back negative for HIV antibodies.

PROFILE: Magic Johnson

Next, Magic held a press conference announcing that he was retiring from basketball to devote his life to teaching people, especially young people, what they needed to know to protect themselves against HIV. He put the same energy, positive attitude, and hard work into his new career as an AIDS activist as he had put into his career as a basketball player. Within the next year, Magic wrote a book entitled *What You Can Do to Avoid AIDS*, made a television special in which he answered teenagers' questions, and eagerly accepted a post on the National Commission on AIDS.

Although he was no longer playing professional basketball, Magic still wanted to be part of the U.S. Olympic basketball team going to Barcelona, Spain, in the summer of 1992. Earlier that year, Magic had been selected to become a member of the NBA All-Star team. He had led the West to an outstanding victory and had received the NBA All-Star Game's Most Valuable Player award.

In January of 1996, Magic returned to the NBA and announced that he would once again play for the Lakers. Fans and teammates alike enthusiastically welcomed him back. In May of 1996, however, they would be disappointed to learn of Magic's decision to retire from professional sports. Earvin "Magic" Johnson remains dedicated to HIV education. Many people believe that he has done more than anyone else to heighten AIDS awareness.

Follow-up Activities

Learn more about Earvin "Magic" Johnson by completing one or more of the following activities. (Information on source books can be found on pages 59.)

1. Describe in your own words Magic's sense of mission as an AIDS activist. (Source: *Sports Illustrated* magazine, November 18, 1991.)

2. Explain the circumstances under which Magic Johnson resigned and later resumed his post on the National Commission on AIDS. (Source: *Magic Johnson: Basketball Wizard.*)

3. In your own words, describe the reaction of most people when they heard Magic's announcement that he had HIV. (Source: *Sports Great: Magic Johnson, Revised and Expanded.*)

4. Write an essay expressing your opinion of Magic Johnson as a role model. Relate what you may have heard him say about HIV and describe the effect of his words on you.

Do I need to worry about HIV if I'm not having sex or using IV drugs?

Even if you are not thinking about having sex yet, or if you believe that you'll never inject a drug into your body, this can be a good time to start thinking about and learning about some of the issues related to sex and drugs. Just as a house needs a strong foundation to last, you need a strong foundation of knowledge and skills in order to deal with the feelings, urges, and pressures involving relationships, sex, and drugs that you may be encountering or will encounter as you become older.

Your foundation will be strong if it is built with facts. You need to have accurate information about sex, drugs, HIV, and other sexually transmitted diseases. Solid feelings of self-esteem and respect for yourself and others, as well as feeling cared for and valued by others, will also be needed to make your foundation strong. Being clear about what you value in your life will enable you to build upon this foundation through sound decision making. In order to put your decisions into practice, however, you will also need to develop skills to express your feelings and needs to others with confidence so that you will be understood and respected.

These things won't just come to you; knowledge must be acquired bit by bit, feelings must be nurtured over time, and skills must be practiced until they feel natural. Unfortunately, some kids have already had experiences that put them at a disadvantage in some of these areas. But everyone can take steps to learn the facts, to deal with difficult feelings and family issues, and to acquire the skills that will help them to make good choices for themselves.

Foundation for Healthy Decisions

(continued)

Knowledge

This book provides an opportunity for you to acquire knowledge about HIV and AIDS. It touches on related topics, such as other STDs, relationships, dating, sex, drugs, and alcohol. These topics may also be covered in your health class and family living class at school. In order to be well-informed, however, you will need much more information on these topics than can possibly be covered in one book or class. Your local or school library can be an excellent source of additional information. Books, audio tapes, and videos are available to help you increase and update your knowledge of HIV/AIDS and related subjects.

Feelings and Attitudes

Self-esteem and respect for others increase your ability to make wise health choices. Many things can increase someone's self-esteem: feeling loved by and important to others, feeling special or unique in some way, feeling strong enough to stand up for yourself, and having good role models—people who have respect for themselves and for others. Identify and spend time with these kinds of people. You may want to look into youth outreach programs, such as Big Brothers or Big Sisters, or other young people's organizations.

Personal and Social Skills

Many skills are needed to deal with the pressures of growing up in today's society. To protect yourself from HIV, you must possess good decision-making, communication, and assertiveness skills. You will need to think clearly about where you want to draw the line on sex and drugs; you will need to communicate your decisions to others; and you will need to have assertiveness and confidence to stick to your decisions.

On Your Own

1. Make three lists:

   a. HIV-related topics that you want to learn more about

   b. your best role models for self-esteem and respect

   c. the personal and social skills that you would like to work on

   Keep these lists private. Refer to them, update them, and act on them often.

2. Find books and videos at your library to help you build your foundation in all three areas. Book and video suggestions can be found on pages 58–60.

How can I be sure that I have accurate facts about sex, HIV, and other STDs?

You may have heard a lot of things about sex from friends. Some of these things may be true and some may not. One of the best ways to make sure that you have accurate information is to find books at your library for your age group about sex and STDs. You may be surprised to learn that there are informative and candid books for kids about these topics. You'll find a few of these books listed on pages 58–59. If someone tells you something or you read something that doesn't seem to fit with what you know, check the library for more information or ask an adult to verify what your friend has told you.

You can ask a parent, your doctor, a school nurse, a teacher, or a counselor questions about sex-related topics. If you feel uneasy or embarrassed to talk to adults about sex, start small by commenting on a current news story or television program, or by asking a less embarrassing question first. Don't be afraid to say that you are embarrassed; admitting you're embarrassed can help to "break the ice." Adults are sometimes embarrassed, too, and your honesty can help put both of you at ease. Talking to your parents can do a lot to build trust. Parents may also be concerned that they don't have all of the answers. This can be an opportunity to find answers together.

If you have a personal issue or question that you're not ready to discuss with anyone you know, you can call one of several hotlines. Two national hotlines are the CDC National HIV/AIDS Hotline and the CDC National Sexually Transmitted Diseases Hotline. The toll-free phone numbers of these hotlines can be found on page 57. You can also look under "AIDS," "Counseling," or "Youth and Teen Services" in the "Community Services" section of your telephone directory.

How do I decide about sex?

You may already have some personal beliefs about sex. Many people choose **abstinence** from sex until they can choose *responsible sex*, that is, until marriage or until they have been in a relationship with someone for a long time and are sure that the relationship is right for them. Many people want to let a relationship grow and become strong before having sex. Others want to wait because they don't *feel* ready.

There are other issues to consider: the possibility of an unplanned pregnancy, and the possibility of contracting HIV infection or another serious, sexually transmitted disease.

Sex between two people who love and respect each other is very special, and nothing said in this book about the risks of having sex is meant to contradict this. But the fact is, in today's society, the consequences of contracting a sexually transmitted disease are serious and can be deadly. The cautions presented here are practical ones, not moral ones.

If you are not sure about how you feel about abstinence, talk it through with someone older whom you respect and trust. Apply what you know about sound decision making to the question of abstinence. Ask yourself: "What are my choices? What are the benefits and risks of each possible choice? What are the possible outcomes of each choice?" With these questions answered, you will be better prepared to make a sound decision.

This is an important decision—one that can affect the rest of your life. By choosing abstinence, in advance, you can help ensure that you won't become overwhelmed by the emotions, desires, or pressures of the moment. You can also protect yourself against possible guilt, loss of self-respect, or loss of trust in another person, as well as against possible unplanned pregnancy and sexually transmitted diseases.

On Your Own

Test the above decision-making questions on the outcomes of some recent decisions you have made. Could the outcomes have been better? How?

How can I stick to my decision to abstain from sex and drugs?

Here are some suggestions for ways to deal with pressures to have sex or use drugs that you may feel from within, from others, or from situations:

- Be aware that the media presents many messages that may entice you to want to have sex. Some of these messages are obvious, but many are subtle. Notice that most television dramas and movies would have you believe that people have multiple encounters of unprotected sex and never contract HIV or any other STD. That is not realistic.

- As you get older, don't buy into the idea that there is something wrong with you if you don't have sex by a certain age, even if some of your peers say they have.

- Remember that you never need to have sex to "prove" your love for someone.

- Also remember that if someone wants to have sex with you, that does not necessarily mean that the person loves you. Having sex doesn't make a bad relationship better; things like caring, honest communication, trust, and respect make a relationship better.

- At some point, you may be tempted to experiment with drugs or alcohol. Or you may find yourself looking for a way out of some emotional pain. There are things you can do to prepare for these situations. For example, you can find other ways to make yourself feel good, and you can plan ahead so you know whom you could talk to about emotional problems before things get worse.

- Understand that using alcohol and drugs can impair your judgment and cause you to temporarily disregard your decision to abstain from sex. If you are intoxicated, you might not stop to think about what your are doing, or you might tell yourself that there is really nothing to worry about. That is dangerous thinking.

On Your Own

1. If you have a healthy relationship and want to share emotional and physical closeness, there are lots of ways to do this besides sexual intercourse. List ten or more ways to be emotionally and physically close without having sex.

2. List ten or more ways to feel good that don't involve using alcohol or drugs.

How can I prepare for resisting pressures to have sex and use drugs?

Being clear about your decisions is not enough; you need to know how to stick to your decisions under pressure. The following situations all involve pressure of one kind or another. Each contains an example of a teen's clear and assertive response to handling this pressure:

- It's summer. Maria and Jason have been seeing each other all through the school year. Maria wants to show her deep feelings for Jason, but she is afraid that she may go too far. She says, "I really care about you, Jason, but I've made a decision not to have sex until I can make a lifelong commitment."

- Lisa has started pressuring her boyfriend, Kurt, to have sex. Lisa asks, "What's wrong, don't you want me?" Kurt says, "Yes, and I want what's right for both of us." Lisa says, "I thought you were attracted to me." Kurt says, "I am, but because of HIV, I'm not going to have sex until marriage."

- At a party, Robert says, "If you loved me, you'd do it." Carrie says, "If you loved me, you wouldn't try to talk me into doing it." Robert continues to pressure Carrie by saying, "I know that you really want to; you just need to relax. Here, have some beer." Carrie says, "I'm going to leave now because I don't like the way you're acting." (Always be prepared to leave; for example, have money for a phone call.)

- Some of Jim's friends are beginning to use drugs. They want him to experiment, too. Kenny says, "Here, Jim, just try it; you'll like it." Steve says, "Come on, Jim. Everyone does it." Jim doesn't want to lose their friendship, but he understands the risks of using drugs. He says, "I want to stay friends with you guys, but I don't want to experiment with drugs."

On Your Own

Write scripts for the above and other situations in which the characters' actions result in abstinence from sex or drugs. Alternate playing the roles with a friend or classmate. By practicing these simulations, you will become more comfortable with saying the words if and when a real-life situation occurs.

Later, when I choose responsible sex, will I need to use protection?

When you are older and in a long-term, committed relationship, you may choose to have responsible sex. Even if you have never had sex or used IV drugs, and your partner tells you that he or she hasn't either, you should still plan on using protection.

The most common type of protection is the latex **condom**, a thin rubber cover placed over the penis before having sex. The condom prevents semen and preseminal fluid from coming in contact with the female and also prevents vaginal fluids from coming in contact with the male. Condoms are *not* 100 percent effective, however; they can tear or slip off.

Next to abstinence, the use of a latex condom and a **spermicidal**, *water-based* lubricant is the best way to protect both partners from HIV infection. Spermicides have been shown to kill HIV, but a spermicide used without a condom offers little or no protection from HIV. The best type of spermicidal, water-based lubricant contains nonoxynol-9.

Latex condoms can also protect against other sexually transmitted diseases and pregnancy. Other forms of birth control, such as the pill, the diaphragm, and the sponge, do not protect against HIV.

Older teens should know where to get latex condoms, what they cost, and how to use them correctly. Having this information can help ensure that a condom will be used if and when responsible sex in a committed relationship is chosen. Condoms are available at drug stores, supermarkets, and convenience stores. County health clinics and planned parenthood clinics sometimes provide them for little or no charge. HIV educators at family planning centers and local health departments, as well as books at the library, can provide instruction and information on how to correctly use condoms.

On Your Own

Not everyone is open to the idea of using condoms. Some people are embarrassed to buy them, some are embarrassed to put one on in front of another person, and some may even fear that their partner suggested using a condom because he or she has HIV. The best way to handle a discussion about condoms with someone who is reluctant to use them is to be patient, assertive, and consistent. With a friend or fellow student, role-play several situations in which you discuss each of these fears.

Are there any other precautions kids need to take against HIV?

There are precautions that you can take in situations that may pose a slight risk under certain circumstances. Ear piercing, tattooing, and acupuncture require the use of needles. If these needles are used on someone who is infected with HIV and then reused on another person, the virus could possibly be passed on through a tiny bit of blood left on the needle.

Sharing personal items, such as razors, toothbrushes, tweezers, or scissors, may also pose a very slight risk because of the chance of blood remaining on them after use.

Here are some precautions you can take to make sure you are not putting yourself at any risk:

- If you get your ears pierced, get tattooed, or see an acupuncturist, be certain that the person performing the service is certified (and licensed, if your state requires it). Also make sure that only new, sterilized, packaged needles are used. Never tattoo yourself or a friend, particularly with the same needle.

- Do not share a razor, tweezers, scissors, toothbrush, or any other item that may contain blood from another person, especially if you have a cut or sore that might come in contact with it. If you need to share one of these items, wash it in soapy water, soak it in bleach for ten minutes, and rinse it under running water for three minutes.

PROFILE: Greg Louganis

Greg Louganis fell in love with the sport of diving at an early age. Greg's father was Samoan, and his mother was an American of North European descent. His young parents were unable to provide for him, however, and he was adopted by Pete and Francis Louganis when he was nine months old. As a young child, Greg developed the qualities of a great diver: athletic ability, strength, and grace. He learned grace through dance lessons, which he began at age three. His mother let him take lessons with his older sister after he had begun trying everything that she did. Soon he was excelling in dancing and gymnastics as well.

When Greg was nine years old, his family put in a backyard swimming pool. Greg immediately began doing flips off the diving board. Rather than forbid him from doing what he loved, his parents decided to give him diving lessons. Greg's childhood was far from perfect, though. He was teased because of his dark skin; he had trouble reading; he stuttered; and he was painfully shy.

When it came to diving, though, Greg didn't let these problems get in his way. Greg practiced his sport every chance he got. When he was only 11 years old, Greg was picked to go to the Junior Olympics in Colorado. At age 13, he competed in Europe against the best junior divers in the world. By the time Greg was a teenager, he was leading a double life. In the sport of diving, he was a star; at school, he was called names such as "sissy" and "retard." Greg coped by carrying his pet boa constrictor around with him and later by smoking and drinking with a rough crowd. Greg's parents became concerned that Greg might be headed for trouble, so they decided to put him in training with Dr. Sammy Lee, a well-known diving coach. Greg went to live with Dr. Lee so that he could spend more time training. He helped earn his way by cleaning the pool and helping with the cooking.

Just one year later, at age 16, Greg was ready for the 1976 Winter Olympics in Montreal, Canada. Greg was younger than the other divers, and they resented him. Greg was used to being shunned; he just ignored them and did his best. He ended up winning the silver medal. In 1978, after a back injury, Greg began to lose interest in diving. He had started using drugs and hanging around with his old smoking and drinking friends again. Luckily, a new coach, Ron O'Brien, helped Greg regain his interest and confidence. Unfortunately for Greg and the other American athletes, the United

PROFILE: Greg Louganis

States refused to participate in the 1980 Olympic Games in Moscow because the Soviet Union had invaded Afghanistan. But Greg's love of diving was stronger than ever, and he decided to keep training for the 1984 games. It turned out to be a good choice. Greg Louganis won two gold medals in 1984 and two more in 1988—something no other diver had ever done.

For anyone who saw the 1988 games, the memory of Greg's victory is special. Greg had hit his head on the springboard during his ninth dive of the preliminaries. Determined to continue, he came back minutes later with four stitches in his head. The crowd held its breath as Greg prepared for an even more difficult dive. He performed it almost perfectly, and placed among the ten finalists.

Greg had won the hearts of all those who watched these events just as much for his courage and determination as for his athletic skill. But what nobody knew was that only a few months before the 1988 Olympic Games, Greg Louganis had tested positive for HIV. He did not publicly acknowledge that he was gay until 1994, nor that he had AIDS until 1995.

Today, Greg breeds and shows Great Danes and promotes AIDS awareness. He also is consulting on a television movie based on his book *Breaking the Surface*.

Follow-up Activities

To learn more about Greg Louganis, complete one or more of the following activities. (See page 59 for more information on the source books.)

1. In high school, Greg discovered why he always had trouble reading. Write a few paragraphs describing Greg's problem and how he overcame it. (Sources: *Greg Louganis: Diving for Gold*, page 46, and *Breaking the Surface*, pages 34–35.)

2. Describe how his success as a diver helped Greg get through an otherwise unhappy and lonely childhood at home and at school. (Source: *Breaking the Surface*, pages 27–45.)

3. Describe how playing a role in the play, *Jeffrey*, helped Greg decide to end his dependence on pain medication and write his autobiography. (Source: *Breaking the Surface*, pages 261–270.)

4. Describe the challenges Greg overcame after announcing that he had AIDS and why he feels that facing the challenges made him a better person. (Source: *The Advocate*, April 4, 1995, page 25.)

How do people get tested for HIV?

People who have had unprotected sex or who have shared needles to inject drugs may be advised by a doctor, nurse, counselor, relative, or friend to get an HIV-antibody test. Sometimes people decide for themselves to get tested because of concerns about their high-risk behavior or because they have been sick, or have had other STDs, for a long time.

Professionals normally refer people to a local testing site. Some people get their own referrals by contacting an HIV counselor at their county health department, local HIV/AIDS service organization, or a local or national HIV/AIDS hotline. These numbers can usually be found in the "Community Services" section of the telephone directory.

HIV counselors are a key element of the testing process. They guide people through the testing process, which can include a wait for results of up to two weeks. They help people deal with their feelings of anxiety, fear, and anger about the possibility of having HIV. They also help people decide whether they want their test results kept private.

There are two ways people can choose to keep their test results private: *anonymous testing* and *confidential testing*. With anonymous testing, which is not available in all states, people do not give their names. They are given a number, and the results are recorded with the number, which only the person being tested knows. With confidential testing, test results are kept private from everyone except medical personnel or, in some states, the state health department.

On Your Own

Obtain more information about HIV-antibody testing from your local health department. Prepare an oral or written report on what you learn.

What does HIV testing show?

HIV testing determines whether or not a person has been infected with HIV, the virus that causes AIDS. At some point between two weeks and six months after HIV enters the bloodstream, the body begins to produce special proteins called antibodies in an effort to weaken and destroy the virus. If HIV antibodies are present in a blood sample taken from a patient, that patient is said to be *HIV-positive*. If HIV antibodies are not present, the patient is said to be *HIV-negative*.

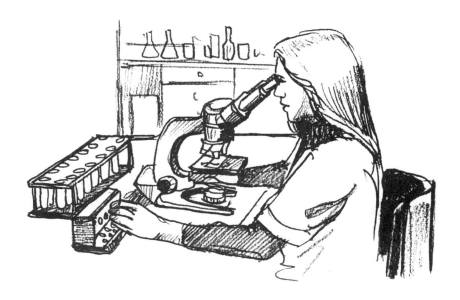

Negative results can, however, turn out to be incorrect, or "false," if a person is tested before the body has a chance to produce HIV antibodies. The two-week to six-month period during which a person could be infected but have no HIV antibodies is called the **window period**.

It is important to understand and remember the window-period concept, because a couple who plans to make a commitment and wants to ensure that neither person has been previously infected, may choose to be tested at the time of their commitment and again six months later. During the time period between the first and second tests, the couple should practice abstinence or at least use a condom and spermicide to protect each other in case one of them was previously infected.

The window-period concept applies to IV drug users as well. An IV drug user would have to test HIV-negative six months after the last time he or she shared a needle to inject an IV drug, or had unprotected sex, to be sure that the negative results were correct.

What do people do next if they test positive for HIV?

People whose test results come back "HIV-positive" are helped by a counselor at the test site to deal with the fear and anger that most people feel when they are told. They are advised to see a doctor as soon as possible. Prompt medical care may delay the onset of AIDS and may prevent some life-threatening diseases. They are also told to abstain from sexual intercourse and to advise any past sex or drug partners that they should be tested.

Life usually becomes very difficult for people infected with HIV, but many overcome the difficulties and go on to help others. People with HIV must change their lifestyles for the rest of their lives. They must live with certain restrictions for the purpose of protecting themselves and others. They must have frequent medical checkups, tests, shots, and medications. They must pay special attention to their health and well-being.

People who test positive for HIV cannot donate blood, organs, sperm, or bone marrow. They must remember not to share any personal items that may have touched their blood, semen, or vaginal fluids. They may decide not to risk having children. If they are married or plan to marry, they need to decide whether to abstain from sex or to take the risks involved in having protected sex. Even if both partners are infected, doctors advise using condoms because condoms offer protection from different strains of HIV and from other STDs, both of which can cause the disease to progress faster.

Many support groups help people with HIV find ways to adjust to the lifestyle changes they will need to make.

Is there a test for AIDS?

AIDS, acquired immune deficiency syndrome, is a set of symptoms which develops as a result of severe damage to the human immune system caused by the virus called HIV. A diagnosis of AIDS is not based on a test, but rather on a *definition* consisting of a set of conditions characteristic of AIDS. These conditions are determined by the Centers for Disease Control and Prevention.

One of the conditions in this definition is based on a test which shows a person's CD4 cell count. CD4 cells are the type of white blood cells that HIV destroys as the virus replicates. These cells are a key part of the immune system because they play a vital role in directing other cells to find and destroy invading microorganisms.

The other conditions of the CDC's definition of AIDS involve more than twenty opportunistic infections and cancers that tend to be rare in the general population, but frequently occur in HIV-infected people.

If an HIV patient's CD4 cell count drops below 200, and he or she has been clinically diagnosed with one or more of the opportunistic infections or AIDS-related cancers listed in the CDC's definition of AIDS, that person is said to have developed AIDS.

On Your Own

Do library research or use the Internet to learn more about the CDC's definition of AIDS and at what point an HIV-positive patient is said to have AIDS.

How do doctors treat patients with HIV and AIDS?

Treating HIV and AIDS patients is difficult and complex. Doctors who treat HIV and AIDS patients receive special training and follow specific guidelines.

They must monitor the effects of HIV on the immune system and prescribe medication at the appropriate times and dosages to maximize results. They must sort out a wide variety of overlapping symptoms and determine which opportunistic infections to treat and how to treat them. They must watch for signs of AIDS-related cancers and determine the best course of treatment. They also must prescribe drugs to lessen the severity of symptoms.

Many people who learn that they have been infected with HIV have no symptoms and have normal CD4 cell counts. They must, however, still have frequent checkups so that the doctors can provide timely treatment as it is needed.

HIV patients are generally advised to eat healthy diets, get regular exercise and plenty of rest, avoid excessive stress, and give up smoking, drinking, or taking drugs. Many HIV/AIDS patients join support groups where they can share information and relate to others who are dealing with the same kinds of emotional issues.

Some doctors help their HIV/AIDS patients enroll as volunteers in "clinical trials," which are tests of new drugs on humans. In clinical trials, some patients get the drug being tested, and others get a placebo (pla-SEE-bo) or "sugar pill," with no drug in it. The results are compared between the two groups, with the hope that the group receiving the medication has shown signs of improvement.

Can HIV infection be stopped?

Yes. HIV infection can be stopped if people find ways to avoid the two high-risk behaviors that allow the virus to pass from one person to another. There is, however, no way to ensure that people guard their own health and the health of others. It is, therefore, up to each individual to do what it takes to overcome the pressures that cause many people to take these risks.

Many medical, social, and educational researchers believe that the only realistic hope for prevention of HIV infection is through educating people about how to avoid high-risk activities. Effective education must involve much more than facts about HIV and AIDS. It must also address the many factors that influence how people behave—peer pressure, media influence, social values, cultural traditions, family and community support, and more.

Effective education must also stress the importance of getting tested for HIV. Testing is essential for anyone who has ever engaged in high-risk activities, such as unprotected sex or sharing needles to inject IV drugs. Everyone who is tested is educated and counseled about how to prevent future HIV infection. Many people who test negative are so grateful that they totally eliminate any high-risk behaviors they may have practiced in the past.

For those who are already infected, it is very likely too late. For IV drug users or sexual partners of drug users, it may also be too late. For people who have had many or several sexual partners but haven't yet been infected, there is still a chance. For you and your peers—members of the young generation who hopefully haven't begun any risky behaviors— there is an opportunity to avoid this virus completely. In fact, you and other people your age may have the biggest effect of any generation so far in stopping this deadly virus in its tracks.

PROFILE: Elizabeth Glaser

You may not recognize Elizabeth Glaser's picture, but you may have heard of her husband, actor Paul Glaser. Paul played detective Starsky in the television series, *Starsky and Hutch*, which ran weekly from 1975 to 1979.

When Elizabeth met Paul in 1975, she was a 27-year-old teacher at a special ungraded school for six- to nine-year-olds in West Hollywood, California. It was love at first sight for both of them. Elizabeth and Paul were married on August 24, 1980. Three months later, Elizabeth was pregnant with their first child, a daughter they named Ariel.

Ariel was born on August 4, 1981. A complication caused Elizabeth to bleed severely. The doctors had to give her seven pints of blood to replace the blood she had lost. Elizabeth recovered, and on October 25, 1984, Ariel's baby brother, Jake, was born with no complications.

About a year after Jake's birth, Ariel began to have stomachaches, diarrhea, and cramps. Then her lips turned white and she began to tire easily. At first, the doctors thought that she had picked up a virus during a trip the family took to Puerto Rico. Later they discovered that her red blood cell count was dangerously low and they became fearful that her kidneys might fail. After about a month in the hospital, Ariel was strong enough to go home, but she was still not well. In late May of 1986, after five months of tests, the doctors learned that Ariel had AIDS.

Elizabeth, Paul, and Jake were tested immediately. Elizabeth and Jake were HIV-positive. Elizabeth had contracted the virus from the blood she received during her hospital stay in 1981 (before blood banks began testing blood for HIV). Paul, miraculously, was not infected. As Ariel began to get worse, Elizabeth decided she had to do something to try to save her children. She looked for AIDS organizations dedicated to helping children, but found none.

Elizabeth did not give up; she believed that not nearly enough was being done for children with AIDS. She began by making lists of every doctor, politician, and celebrity she could think of who might be able to help. Then she started asking influential people to help her set up meetings. Within six weeks, Elizabeth was speaking to the head of the President's Commission on AIDS and meeting with several other AIDS experts in Washington, D.C. Elizabeth asked them why there was such a delay in getting AZT to children, why the federal budget for experimental drugs for children was so small, and why they didn't know how children became infected with HIV. They had no answers because no one had ever asked.

Little came of Elizabeth's questions and desire to help. She did, however, learn of intravenous AZT and was able to get this treatment for Ariel. It reversed some of her brain damage, and Ariel was again able to speak and walk. Next, Elizabeth met with President and Mrs. Reagan. Her story touched the Reagans, and the President promised that he would help. Not much happened, though, because of governmental "red tape." Elizabeth decided that things might happen quicker through a private foundation.

By the summer of 1988, Ariel's illness was worse again. This time nothing helped. On August 12th, seven-year-old Ariel died. With the pain of her daughter's death still weighing heavy on her heart, Elizabeth renewed her mission of promoting pediatric AIDS research. At Ariel's funeral, she met Paul's wealthy aunt, Vera, who gave Elizabeth $500,000 to help start her foundation. Elizabeth immediately contacted her friends, Susan DeLaurentis and Susie Zeegen. Together they founded the Pediatric AIDS Foundation, which continues to fund and conduct basic pediatric AIDS research. The foundation became Elizabeth's hope for her son, Jake, who was then four years old.

Elizabeth Glaser died on December 3, 1994. At that time, Jake was 10 years old and still asymptomatic. Elizabeth is remembered nationwide as a courageous and unselfish woman who, in the face of her own illness, put all her energy into trying to save her children. Her efforts continue to help all children infected with HIV.

Follow-up Activities

Do research to answer the following questions about Elizabeth Glaser. (More information on the source book can be found on page 59.)

1. Why had the Glasers wanted to keep their story from the public? What discovery prompted the Glasers to contact the *Los Angeles Times* with their story? (Source: *In the Absence of Angels*, pages 254 and 259–261.)

2. What did former President Reagan do after he read the Glasers' story in the *Los Angeles Times*? (Source: *In the Absence of Angels*, pages 272–274, 291, and 297.)

3. What program, sponsored by the Pediatric AIDS Foundation, prevents HIV infection in unborn babies? (Source: *People* magazine, December 19, 1994, page 53.)

4. What lesson did Elizabeth Glaser say she learned from AIDS? (Source: *In the Absence of Angels*, pages 296–297.)

What are national agencies doing to help?

Agencies and institutes of the federal government, such as the CDC, and many national nonprofit organizations and foundations conduct HIV/AIDS research, test new drugs, provide literature on prevention and treatment, sponsor public awareness campaigns, staff hotlines, and more.

Certain days are set aside to help bring AIDS issues to the public's attention and to raise funds for treatment and prevention. The National Day of Compassion (June 21) and World AIDS Day (December 1) are two of these days. The first World AIDS Day was observed in 1988.

The Names Project AIDS Memorial Quilt and AIDS red ribbons are special AIDS symbols that have helped to keep AIDS awareness alive in this country. The AIDS quilt was started in the spring of 1987 and was first displayed in October of that year in Washington, D.C. It now contains more than 33,000 panels made and donated by people in remembrance of loved ones who have died from AIDS. Parts of the quilt are still displayed at various events across the country. Many people also wear red ribbons in honor of friends or relatives who have died from AIDS.

State and county health departments also provide education and prevention programs, anonymous testing, counseling, prevention campaigns for the media, educational pamphlets, hotlines, care facilities, and more.

On Your Own

1. Look for newspaper articles on World AIDS Day. What are some of the ways different countries observe this day?

2. Ask a local AIDS service organization if the AIDS Memorial Quilt will be displayed in your area, or do research to find pictures of it in books at your library or on the Internet at http://www.aidsquilt.org.

What are community groups doing to help?

Community centers offer HIV prevention programs designed to meet particular community needs. Many of these programs are geared to young people. Trained, sensitive HIV educators make presentations to schools, churches and synagogues, and youth organizations. Some HIV prevention programs are designed to reach people who live in areas where drug use is high.

Youth organizations, schools, and other community groups help kids overcome fears of being around people who have HIV or AIDS. They also help kids deal with any confusion about their own emerging sexual orientation. Some of these organizations provide assistance in situations involving discrimination against homosexuals, bisexuals, and people with HIV or AIDS.

Communities organize events such as AIDS walks to raise money for local AIDS service organizations that help people with HIV and AIDS pay for housing and medical care. In addition, local organizations often provide support groups, nursing care, hospices, or group homes.

In one small town, a dozen restaurants donated 10% of their profits on World AIDS Day to the local AIDS support organization to help pay for the education programs and services they provide to local residents with AIDS and HIV. The restaurants used the slogan, "Eat Out—Save Lives." Other cities organize marches or parades, candlelight vigils, AIDS Quilt ceremonies, or artistic performances on World AIDS Day.

What can kids do to help?

There are many things that kids can do to help in the fight against HIV, both on a personal level and on a community level. Here are a few suggestions for ways that you can prepare yourself to make a difference in the fight against HIV:

- Make sure that you have accurate facts about HIV and AIDS so that you don't mislead others—or yourself!

- Ask yourself if you are fearful when you think about being around someone with HIV or AIDS. If you are, determine exactly what it is that you're afraid of. Then ask yourself whether this fear is realistic. For example, if you fear sharing a soda with a friend who has HIV, ask yourself, "Is it possible to catch HIV that way?"

- Think about the possibility of one of your friends contracting HIV. Ask yourself if you would continue to be a friend to this person. Would you still include him or her in the activities that you shared before? Would you encourage him or her to eat properly, get enough rest, and stay away from drugs and alcohol? Remember that a person with HIV needs to know he or she is cared about in order to try to remain healthy.

- Ask yourself if you can communicate to a friend the importance of abstaining from sex and drugs to protect himself or herself against HIV.

How Kids Can Help
(continued)

There are also many ways that kids can help in community efforts to fight HIV. Here are some suggestions:

- Encourage your family and friends to participate in local fundraisers or AIDS awareness events on World AIDS Day, National Compassion Day, and at other times your community may designate as AIDS awareness week or month.

- Volunteer to help organize an AIDS awareness or fundraising event at your school or youth group. You might suggest a car wash, a barbecue, or an ice cream or bake sale.

- Call your local AIDS service organization and volunteer to provide assistance to people with AIDS in need of help with household chores, yard work, or errands.

- Help educate peers or younger kids about HIV/AIDS. Learn about peer education opportunities at your school, local AIDS service organization, county health department, or other community health agencies.

- Donate your time or help raise funds for an organization that helps young people who have AIDS. Here are a few suggestions:

AIDS Orphan Adoption Project
1-800-333-6232

Camp Heartland
(a summer camp for kids with AIDS)
1-800-724-HOPE (4673)

National Pediatric HIV Resource Center
Children's Hospital of New Jersey
1-800-362-0071

Pediatric AIDS Foundation
(basic research and funding for children with AIDS)
1311 Colorado Avenue
Santa Monica, CA 90404

Ronald McDonald House
(temporary residential facilities for families with children in hospitals)
Call directory assistance to locate the facility nearest you.

Ryan White Children's Education Fund
Omer Foust, c/o James W. Riley Memorial Association
50 S. Meridian Street, Suite 500
Indianapolis, IN 46204

Extended Activities

Research

1. Look under the "AIDS" heading in the "Community Services" section of your telephone directory. Call three of the numbers and ask for information about their services. List three services provided by each. Keep this list in your telephone directory.

2. Find newspaper or magazine articles that discuss mandatory HIV testing. Learn under what conditions HIV testing is required by law. Write an essay explaining whether you agree or disagree with mandatory testing and why.

3. Call your community center, health department, family planning clinic, or other local HIV education source and ask for HIV prevention brochures directed to people in your age group. Find out if they do presentations at schools. If they do, ask your teacher to invite them to come to your school.

Writing

1. Write an essay on abstinence, beginning with one of these sentences:
   a. Having sex should be based on a carefully-made decision, not because you are pressured into it.
   b. Respecting the wishes of your girlfriend or boyfriend is a good reason for abstinence.

2. Write a poem or short story about discrimination against people with HIV/AIDS or about some of the myths related to HIV and AIDS.

3. Write a letter expressing your support to a friend, real or fictional, who has contracted HIV.

4. Write an essay on the advantages and disadvantages of being tested for HIV.

Art

1. Design a poster encouraging kids your age to avoid the behaviors that can lead to HIV infection.

2. Think of a theme for a new AIDS awareness event, then create a flyer to announce it.

3. Design an AIDS awareness postage stamp.

Extended Activities

(continued)

Drama and Role-Play

With help from a teacher or counselor, use the following guidelines for some three-minute drama and role-playing exercises followed by group comments:

- Allow the players to describe how they felt as they played their roles.

- Limit audience comments to constructive suggestions on what other things a character might have said in the situation.

- Do not judge the quality of a player's performance.

- Respect the privacy of the players if they happen to reveal something personal. You may want to prepare written scripts at first and then try some improvisations, but be sure to limit the dialogue to the situation and each character's position.

Here are some suggested situations to role play:

1. Michelle and Mark, both age 13, have been seeing each other for more than a year. They are beginning to have sexual feelings for one another. Michelle has made a decision not to have sex until she marries, but Mark hasn't really thought about it. He is about to start pressuring Michelle. Michelle decides it is time to talk to Mark about her decision. Because she cares about him so much, she explains her decision, how she arrived at it, and why it is important. She asks him to respect her decision.

2. Shandra is 13 and she really likes Dwayne, who is 14. Shandra thinks that she will have to be willing to have sex with Dwayne to have him as a boyfriend. Shandra's older sister, Tasha, who is 16, encourages her to do what is right for her, not for Dwayne. Tasha tells Shandra to list her reasons for having sex with Dwayne and to list the risks involved. Tasha also relates her own experience at age 15 when having sex resulted in pregnancy and she had to make the difficult decision of giving her baby up for adoption.

Extended Activities

(continued)

Drama and Role-Play (continued)

3. Chris and John have been friends since fourth grade. Now, in seventh grade, John has some new friends who are experimenting with drugs. John invites Chris to a party. Chris doesn't want to go and decides to use what he's learned about assertiveness: (1) He states his position without giving reasons or excuses. (2) He keeps repeating his position. (3) When the pressure still doesn't stop, he refuses to discuss it any further.

4. Sarah and Chad have decided to abstain from having sex, but Chad has begun to subtly pressure Sarah. He uses every line in the book. Sarah is challenged to respond to every one of them. Finally, she tells him, "If you don't stop pressuring me, I'm going to break up with you." He doesn't stop; she breaks up with him.

5. Susan and Roberto are both in seventh grade. Susan has a crush on Roberto. She wants him to be her boyfriend. Roberto likes Susan a lot, but he just wants to be good friends. The situation is getting difficult for Roberto because Susan keeps saying things about her feelings for him and flirting with him. This makes Roberto feel uncomfortable. He decides that if he doesn't tell her how he feels, she might think  that he shares her feelings. He tells her, "Susan, I really like being around you, and we always have fun, but I'm starting to feel that you want more. And because I like you so much, I don't want to mislead you. I can't be your boyfriend, but I still want to be good friends."

6. Eric feels shy and awkward in social situations. His parents drink alcohol "to relax." He thinks that if he drinks alcohol or smokes marijuana, he'll be more relaxed and more fun to be around. He knows the dangers of drugs and alcohol, but he is tempted to try them anyway. He remembers that it was easy to talk to Ms. Clayton, his health teacher last year. Eric decides to talk to her and ask her whether she knows of a counselor or program that might help him work through this dilemma.

Extended Activities

(continued)

Peer Discussion

1. Discuss with a group of your friends their reactions to the way the media treats sex. Compare thoughts and feelings about whether sex is portrayed mostly in healthy ways or unhealthy ways.

2. Read a library book for kids about HIV, AIDS, STDs, sex, or drugs. Tell your classmates why you liked or disliked the book. Then read a book someone else liked.

3. Some people feel that the large amount of money needed for upkeep of the AIDS Memorial Quilt could be put to better use. Do you agree or disagree? If you agree, what are some ways you think the money should be spent?

Debate

1. Plan a debate around this question: Should people who test positive for HIV be required to tell their schools or places of employment?

2. Organize a debate to discuss these issues: Does HIV education that involves how to use condoms cause more kids to have sex at earlier ages? Do condom distribution programs encourage kids to have sex at earlier ages? Be prepared to cite studies that support your view.

3. Debate with friends whether states should allow a person to sue someone for giving him or her a sexually transmitted disease. If so, under what circumstances? If not, why not?

4. Debate whether needle-exchange programs for IV drug users should be funded by the government. Begin by researching the history of this controversy. Why do you think federal funding has been unsuccessful so far?

Resources for More Information

Many organizations help people learn about HIV/AIDS prevention and provide support to people who have HIV/AIDS. The following pages list some of these organizations. Also listed are some of the many available books, articles, and videotapes about HIV/AIDS and people who have been diagnosed with HIV/AIDS.

For Information

Many agencies, associations, and foundations furnish AIDS information and services, usually at no cost, to anyone who asks.

AIDS Action Council
1875 Connecticut Ave., N.W., Suite 700
Washington, D.C. 20009

AIDS Clinical Trials Information Service
P.O. Box 6421
Rockville, MD 20849-6421

American Foundation for AIDS Research
733 Third Ave., Twelfth Floor
New York, NY 10017-3204

American Red Cross
Distribution of Materials
Office of HIV/AIDS Education
1709 New York Ave., N.W., Suite 208
Washington, D.C. 20006

American Social Health Association
P.O. Box 13827
Research Triangle Park, NC 27709
(herpes information)

Canadian Public Health Association
AIDS Education Awareness Program
National AIDS Clearinghouse
1565 Carling Ave., Suite 400
Ottawa, Ontario, Canada K1Z 8R1

CDC National AIDS Clearinghouse*
P.O. Box 6003
Rockville, MD 20849-6003
1-800-458-5231

Food and Drug Administration
Press Office, 5600 Fishers Lane
Rockville, MD 20857
BBS: 1-800-222-0185

HIV/AIDS Treatment Information Service
P.O. Box 6303
Rockville, MD 20849-6303
1-800-448-0440 (U.S. & Canada)

National Institutes of Health
Office of AIDS Research (OAR)
Building 31, Room 5C-06
Bethesda, MD 20892

Sexual Minority Youth Assistance League
333 1/2 Pennsylvania Ave., S.E., Third Floor
Washington, D.C. 20003-1148
e-mail: smyal@AOL.com

Sexuality Information and Education
Council of the U.S. (SIECUS)
130 West 42nd St., Suite 2500
New York, NY 10036
(peer education)

---

* The National AIDS Clearinghouse is the largest
source of AIDS information in the country.

Resources for More Information
(continued)

For Answers, Help, and Support

If you have questions that are not answered in the literature or need help or support for yourself, a friend, or family member—or if you're just not sure what to do or whom to call—call one of the following hotlines. These hotlines are staffed with patient, sensitive, and caring people whose only job is to help callers.

You can also look in your telephone directory under "AIDS" in the "Community Services" section near the front of the book. This section usually lists local AIDS service organizations, the health department, and local hotlines.

In addition, each state has an HIV/AIDS hotline. You can get the 800 number for the one in your state by calling the CDC National HIV/AIDS Hotline at one of the numbers provided below.

AIDS and Cancer Research Foundation Hotline
1-800-373-4572

AIDS Hotline for Teens
1-800-234-TEEN (8336)
(staffed by teens 2 PM – 6 PM, PST)

AIDS Project Los Angeles
1-213-993-1600

American Institute for Teen AIDS Prevention
1-817-237-0230

CDC National HIV/AIDS Hotline
1-800-342-AIDS (2437)
1-800-344-7432 (Spanish)
1-800-243-7889 (hearing impaired)

CDC National Sexually Transmitted Diseases Hotline
1-800-227-8922

Covenant House Nine Line
1-800-999-9999
(crisis counseling)

Gay Men's Health Crisis (GMHC)
1-212-807-6655
1-212-645-7470 (hearing impaired)

HIV/AIDS Treatment Information Service
1-800-448-0440
1-800-243-7012 (hearing impaired)

National Association of People with AIDS
1-202-898-0414

National Drug and Alcohol Treatment Routing Service
1-800-662-HELP (4357)

National Herpes Hotline
1-919-361-8488

NO/AIDS Hotline
1-504-945-4000
(parent education)

Project Inform
1-800-822-7422
(treatment information only)

Sexual Minority Youth Assistance League
1-202-546-5940, extension 8
(7 PM – 10 PM, EST)

Resources for More Information
(continued)

Suggested Literature

Public libraries and schools have a variety of materials on HIV, AIDS, sexuality, and drugs. Books for young adults on HIV and AIDS are found under 616.97, books on sexuality for kids are found under 306.70, and books on drug use are found under 362.29. A few excellent examples are

100 Questions and Answers About AIDS: A Guide for Young People, Michael Thomas Ford, Macmillan Publishing Company, New York, NY, 1992.

Abstinence: Teacher/Student Resource (for grades 5–9), ETR Associates, 1-800-321-4407, Santa Cruz, CA, 1996.

AIDS: What Teens Need to Know (for grades 9–12), Barbara Christie-Dever, The Learning Works, Santa Barbara, CA, 1995.

Asking About Sex and Growing Up, Joanna Cole, William Morrow and Company, Inc., New York, NY, 1988.

Be Smart About Sex: Facts for Young People, Jean Fiedler and Hal Fiedler, Ph.D., Enslow Publishers, Inc., Hillside, NJ, 1990.

Boys and Sex, Wardell B. Pomeroy, Ph.D., Dell Publishing, New York, NY, 1991.

Coping Through Self-Esteem, Rhoda McFarland, The Rosen Publishing Group, Inc., New York, NY, 1993.

Different Drummer: Homosexuality in America, Elaine Landau, Julian Messner Division of Simon & Schuster, New York, NY, 1986.

Dr. Ruth Talks to Kids, Dr. Ruth Westheimer, Macmillan Publishing Company, New York, NY, 1993.

Drugs: Teacher/Student Resource, Comprehensive Health for the Middle Grades Series, ETR Associates, 1-800-321-4407, Santa Cruz, CA, 1996.

Girls and Sex, Wardell B. Pomeroy, Ph.D., Dell Publishing, New York, NY, 1991

The How To Book of Teen Self Discovery: Helping Teens Find Balance, Security & Esteem, Doc Lew Childre, Planetary Publication, Boulder Creek, CA, 1992.

Lynda Madaras Talks to Teens about AIDS, Lynda Madaras, Newmarket Press, New York, NY, 1988.

Risky Times: How to be AIDS-Smart and Stay Healthy, Jeanne Blake, Workman Publishing Company, New York, NY, 1990.

Sex Can Wait: A Middle School Program, developed by the University of Arkansas, published by ETR Associates, 1-800-321-4407, Santa Cruz, CA, 1994.

Understanding Sexual Identity: A Book for Gay Teens and Their Friends, Janice Rench, Lerner, 1990.

Resources for More Information
(continued)

Suggested Literature (continued)

Biographies and novels for young adults about people with AIDS are found under 362.19. Here are some that might interest you:

Arthur Ashe and His Match with History, Robert Quackenbush, Simon & Schuster, New York, NY, 1994.

Breaking the Surface, Greg Louganis with Eric Marcus, Random House, Inc., 1995.

Days of Grace: A Memoir, Arthur Ashe and Arnold Rampersad, Alfred A. Knopf, Inc., New York, NY, 1993.

Greg Louganis: Diving for Gold, Joyce Milton, Random House, Inc., New York, NY, 1989.

The Eagle Kite, Paula Fox, Orchard Books, New York, NY, 1995. A novel about a 13-year-old boy who learns that his father has AIDS.

In the Absence of Angels, Elizabeth Glaser and Laura Palmer, G. P. Putnam's Sons, New York, NY, 1991.

Magic Johnson: Basketball Wizard, Martin Schwabacher, Chelsea House Publishers, 1993.

Ryan White: My Own Story, Ryan White and Ann Marie Cunningham, Dial Books, Division of Penguin Books USA, Inc., 1991. Abridged version also available on cassette.

Sports Great, Magic Johnson, Revised and Expanded, James Haskins, Enslow Publishers, Inc., Hillside, NJ, 1992.

Teens with AIDS Speak Out, Mary Kittredge, Thorndike Press, Thorndike, ME, 1991. True stories of teenagers with AIDS.

Thanksgiving: An AIDS Journal, Elizabeth Cox, Harper & Row Publishers, New York, NY, 1990. A moving journal of a young wife and mother whose husband has AIDS.

Until Whatever, Martha Humphreys, Houghton Mifflin Company, Boston, MA, 1991. A novel about a high school student's struggle with HIV and her friend's struggle with fear and social pressure.

We Have AIDS, Elaine Landau, Franklin Watts, Inc., New York, NY, 1990. True stories of teenagers with AIDS.

Also check the *Reader's Guide to Periodical Literature* for the most current HIV and AIDS information. Here is one journal article written especially for adolescents:

"AIDS: From Confusion to Compassion," K. Dowd, *Youth 94*, May-June 1994, 16–19.

Resources for More Information

(continued)

Suggested Videos

Many excellent videos have been produced on HIV/AIDS education, abstinence, communication, self-esteem, and decision making. Some are available through libraries and schools. Here are a few made especially for preteens and young teens. If your library or school does not have them, they are available from the sources listed.

101 Ways to Make Love Without Doin' It (grades 6–12), ETR Associates, 1-800-321-4407, Santa Cruz, CA, 1996.

Between You and Me: Learning to Communicate (grades 5–9), video and teacher's guide, Sunburst Communications, Inc., 1-800-321-7511, Pleasantville, NY, 1991.

I Like Being Me: Self-Esteem (grades 5–9), video and teacher's guide, Sunburst Communications, 1990.

Postponing Sexual Involvement (one for preteens and one for young teens), video and manual, ETR Associates, 1996.

Project SNAPP: Skill and Knowledge for AIDS and Pregnancy Prevention (grades 5–9), a 13-minute trigger video and 100-page curriculum, including eight 45-minute HIV-prevention skills practice sessions, developed by Division of Adolescent Medicine, Children's Hospital, Los Angeles, CA, 1995, available from ETR Associates.

Real People: Teens Who Choose Abstinence (grades 7–12), Sunburst Communications, 1994.

Respect and You (grades 5–9), video and teacher's guide, Sunburst Communications, 1995.

Say No and Keep Your Friends (grades 5–9), video and teacher's guide, Sunburst Communications, 1994.

Speaking of Sex, Big Changes, Big Choices Video Series for Middle School, ETR Associates, 1993.

Teens Talk AIDS (grades 7–12), includes a 195-page informational paperback and discussion guide, ETR Associates, 1992.

Time Out: The Truth About HIV, AIDS, and You (grades 7–12), features Magic Johnson, (free rental available from participating video rental stores), Paramount, 1992.

Update: Sexually Transmitted Diseases and *Teenage Sex: Resisting the Pressure* (grades 7–12), videocassettes and booklets, Sunburst Communications, 1995.

Values and Choices Master Set (grades 7–8), a comprehensive sexuality education program (video, teacher's guide, and parent's guide) that advocates abstinence for young teens, ETR Associates, 1991-1992.

Yes? No? Maybe? Decision-Making Skills (grades 5–9), video and teacher's guide, Sunburst Communications, 1990.

Glossary

abstinence   the act of deliberately and consistently refraining from doing something that one might otherwise be inclined to do

acquired immune deficiency syndrome (AIDS)   a deadly disease caused by the human immunodeficiency virus; *acquired* refers to the fact that the virus infects a person as a result of exposure, rather than heredity

AIDS   acronym standing for acquired immune deficiency syndrome

AIDS-related cancers   certain cancers that are more common in people infected with HIV; AIDS-related cancers include cancers of the lymphatic system (a part of the immune system), anogenital cancers that affect the anus or cervix (the entrance to a female's womb), and Kaposi's sarcoma

anal   of or relating to the anus, the opening between the buttocks

antibodies   substances produced by the blood to neutralize toxins and to weaken or destroy disease-causing microorganisms

antiretroviral drug   a type of drug that works by stopping a virus from replicating

asymptomatic   a term used to describe an initial stage of HIV infection during which there are no symptoms; an asymptomatic person is still able to transmit the disease to others

bisexual   a person who is sexually attracted to both males and females

CD4 cell   the type of lymphocyte that HIV destroys; also called T-helper cell and T4 cell

condom   a sheath, made of latex, which is worn over the penis during sexual intercourse to prevent pregnancy and transmission of sexual transmitted diseases

contract   to acquire a disease through infection

fungi   a class of plant-like organisms, including yeasts and molds; some fungi cause opportunistic infections in people with HIV

genetically   pertaining to genes, the parts of cells that determine the inherited characteristics of an organism or microorganism

heterosexual   a person who is sexually attracted to members of the opposite sex

Glossary
(continued)

HIV   acronym standing for human immunodeficiency virus

HIV antibody test   a laboratory test that counts the HIV antibodies in a person's blood to determine if a person has been infected with HIV

HIV illness   the stage of HIV infection when symptoms usually begin to increase; this is the pre-AIDS stage

homosexual   a person who is sexually attracted to members of the same sex; homosexual males (and females) are commonly called gays; homosexual females are also called lesbians

human immunodeficiency virus (HIV)   a virus that invades and destroys white blood cells, especially CD4 cells

immune   having a high resistance to a disease-causing microorganism

immune system   the complex functions of certain cells and organs of the body that work together to recognize foreign substances and neutralize them

immune system deficiency   a state of the body in which the immune system is lacking what it needs to perform its normal functions

immunomodulator   any substance, but usually refers to a drug, that influences the immune system

intravenous   within, or entering by way of, a person's vein

Kaposi's sarcoma (KS)   a rare form of skin cancer common in some AIDS patients

lubricant   a substance, preferably a water-based cream, that is used to moisten a male's penis, a female's vagina, or a person's anus before sexual intercourse

lymphocyte   a type of white blood cell that aids in the body's immune response; T cells and B cells are types of lymphocytes; CD4 cells are a type of T cell

Glossary
(continued)

microorganism   a minute living body not perceptible to the naked eye; examples include bacteria, fungi, parasites, and viruses

mucous membrane   the thin, inner lining of certain body cavities and passages, such as the mouth, nose, throat, vagina, and rectum

mutate   to change form genetically; HIV, for example, mutates into numerous strains, or varieties, of the virus

opportunistic infection (OI)   one of many infections which usually do not cause illness in a healthy person, but which can cause severe illness in a person who is immune deficient

oral sex   sexual activity in which a person's mouth or tongue comes into contact with a male's penis, a female's vagina, or a person's anus

parasite   an organism that lives within, upon, or at the expense of another organism known as its host

phagocyte   a type of white blood cell that has the ability to ingest and destroy disease-causing microorganisms and other particles

***Pneumocystis carinii* pneumonia (PCP)**   an opportunistic lung infection caused by a parasite, to which people with AIDS are unusually susceptible

preseminal fluid   a lubricating fluid secreted at the tip of the penis after a male is sexually aroused

replicate   to make an exact copy of

semen   the whitish fluid containing male reproductive cells that is produced by males and ejaculated during sexual intercourse or masturbation

sexual intercourse   usually refers to insertion of the penis into the vagina, anus, or mouth

sexual orientation   term used to refer to a person's attraction to the opposite sex, same sex, or both sexes (see also *heterosexual*, *homosexual*, and *bisexual*)

Glossary

(continued)

sexually transmitted disease (STD) a disease acquired as a result of sexual contact with an infected person; examples include chlamydia, genital warts, gonorrhea, Hepatitis B, herpes, HIV/AIDS, syphilis, and vaginitis

spermicide a preparation, usually a cream, used to kill sperm

symptom a physical, mental, or emotional change that a person notices as a sign of illness, such as fever, pain, rash, or depression

syndrome a specific combination of symptoms, indicating the presence of a particular disease or condition

thrush a yeast infection that affects the mouth and throat, producing a whitish coating or spots

transmission passage from one person to another of a disease-causing microorganism

tuberculosis (TB) an opportunistic bacterial infection spread by repeated exposure to airborne droplets from the coughs or sneezes of a person who has TB

vaccine a preparation containing small quantities of live or dead viruses, or some part of them, given to establish resistance to an infection

vaginal secretion fluid released by the lining of the vagina that makes it moist

virus a disease-causing microorganism that depends on a living host in order to replicate; viruses make a host cell behave abnormally

white blood cells the type of blood cells that fights against infection and tissue damage; lymphocytes and phagocytes are types of white blood cells

window period the two-week to six-month period during which a person could be infected with HIV but have no HIV antibodies

yeasts certain single-celled fungi that can cause opportunistic infections

AIDS: Answers to Questions Kids Ask
© The Learning Works, Inc.